what would you ask?
FERDINAND MAGELLAN

Anita Ganeri
Illustrated by Janek Matysiak

Thameside Press

Distributed in the United States by
Smart Apple Media
123 South Broad Street
Mankato, Minnesota 56001

Text copyright © Anita Ganeri 1999

Editors: Veronica Ross & Claire Edwards
Designer: Simeen Karim
Illustrator: Janek Matysiak
Consultant: Hester Collicutt

Printed in China

ISBN: 1-929298-02-1
Library of Congress Catalog Card Number 99-73400

10 9 8 7 6 5 4 3 2 1

Contents

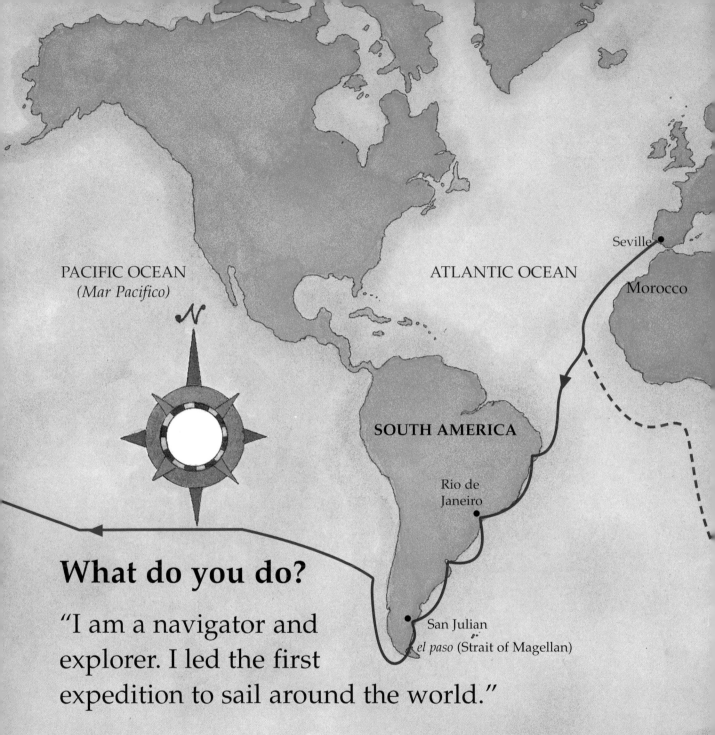

PACIFIC OCEAN
(Mar Pacifico)

ATLANTIC OCEAN

Seville

Morocco

SOUTH AMERICA

Rio de
Janeiro

San Julian
el paso (Strait of Magellan)

What do you do?

"I am a navigator and
explorer. I led the first
expedition to sail around the world."

On September 20, 1519, Ferdinand Magellan set out on one of the most
famous journeys ever made. His dream was to find a new sea route to
the Spice Islands. Like most explorers, Magellan was motivated by trade
with countries in the East, such as China and India. Any country that
could discover a new trade route would gain great wealth and power.

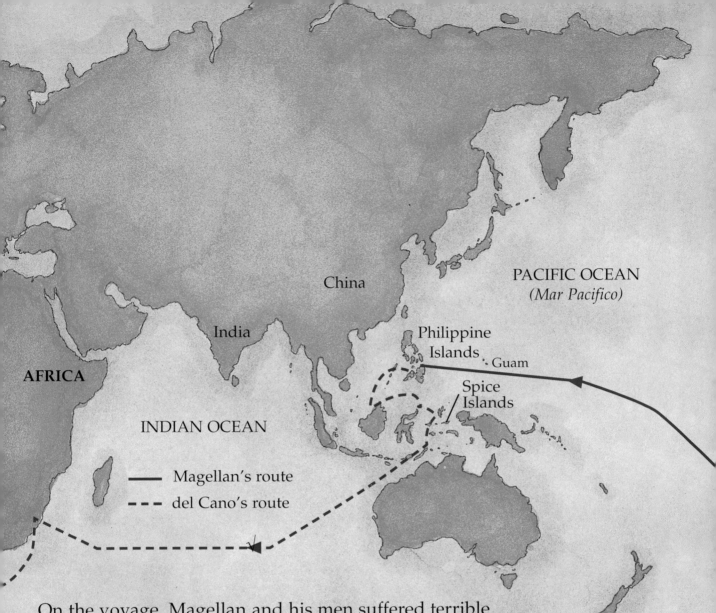

China

PACIFIC OCEAN
(Mar Pacifico)

India

Philippine
Islands

Guam

AFRICA

Spice
Islands

INDIAN OCEAN

—— Magellan's route

--- del Cano's route

On the voyage, Magellan and his men suffered terrible
hardships. Their ships were wrecked by storms. They were
driven mad by hunger, thirst, and disease. Yet, spurred on by
Magellan's skill and leadership, they became the first Europeans
to sail across the Pacific Ocean, proving that the Earth was round.

Magellan did not live to complete the journey, and his ship
finally returned to Spain without him. At the time, Magellan's
achievements were not taken seriously. It wasn't until long after
his death that people gave him the respect he deserved.

Where and when were you born?

"I was born in Portugal in 1480."

Ferdinand Magellan was probably born in Sabrosa, Portugal, in the spring of 1480. His parents were wealthy nobles. Ferdinand grew up in the family farmhouse, an old, rambling place with cows, goats, and chickens.

At the age of seven, Ferdinand was sent to school in a nearby monastery. He learnt about his Catholic faith here and studied Latin and math. But he really preferred to be out in the fresh air with his brothers.

When he was twelve, Ferdinand was sent to the court at Lisbon to become a page. He learned music, dancing, swordplay, and hunting—all the skills he needed to serve at court. But he was also taught astronomy, mapmaking, and navigation. These were the skills that would shape Ferdinand's whole life.

Did you always want to be a sailor?

"Yes, even as a child I longed to go to sea."

At court, Ferdinand heard many stories of the daring explorers who sailed the Atlantic and Indian Oceans, opening up new trade routes to the East. The most famous explorer of all was Vasco da Gama.

In 1499, when Ferdinand was 19, da Gama sailed back to Lisbon with a cargo of spices, pearls, and silks from the East. On his journey, he had discovered a sea route to India. This discovery turned Portugal into one of the wealthiest countries in Europe. Lisbon became a thriving port, lined with docks, shipyards, and warehouses. Every day, ships arrived from all over the world to unload their cargos.

Ferdinand longed to go to sea. He, too, wanted to make his fortune and see the world.

Where did you go on your first voyage?

"I sailed to Africa and India and then on to the Spice Islands. Then I sailed to the Philippine Islands."

In Ferdinand's time, the trade in spices, such as pepper, ginger, and cloves, was very important. This trade was mainly controlled by Arab traders, who brought spices to Europe from the East. King Manuel of Portugal decided to send a fleet to challenge the Arabs at sea. Ferdinand asked permission to join one of the ships.

The king agreed and on March 25, 1505, at the age of 25, Ferdinand went to sea. He fought many battles and was badly wounded. But he was more interested in exploration than fighting, so he joined an expedition traveling east to the Spice Islands. From there, he sailed on to the Philippine Islands, at the very limits of the known world.

On each voyage, Ferdinand showed that he was a skilled sailor, as well as a brave, fair, and honest leader. He returned to Portugal as an experienced sea captain.

What was your most famous voyage?

"In 1519, I set sail westward to the Spice Islands. This was to be my greatest voyage."

Ferdinand wanted to reach the Spice Islands by sailing west instead of east. At that time, people thought that a great land mass blocked the way to the west. But John of Lisbon, a navigator and a friend of Ferdinand's, claimed to have found a way through.

John called his discovery *el paso*—the passage. He wanted Ferdinand to find *el paso*, but first, Ferdinand needed a sponsor. King Manuel refused to pay for his voyage. So in October 1517, Ferdinand left Portugal for the court of Charles I, the king of Spain. Charles welcomed Ferdinand and agreed to help him.

In 1493, Spain and Portugal had agreed a treaty. All lands east of a line through the Atlantic belonged to Portugal. Lands to the west belonged to Spain. Portugal also controlled the eastward sea route to the Spice Islands. By sailing west, Magellan hoped to find a new route, with all the wealth and glory that would bring.

How many ships did you take?

"We took five ships, including the *Trinidad*, my flagship."

Magellan was given five ships for his expedition—the *Trinidad*, *San Antonio*, *Concepçion*, *Victoria*, and *Santiago*. Conditions on board were cramped, and the ships were crawling with cockroaches, lice, and rats. In Seville, a lot of work was needed before the ships were seaworthy. Rotten wood had to be replaced, new sails were fitted, and the hulls were cleaned and made waterproof.

Supplies consisted of food and drink, general equipment, such as nails and canvases, weapons, and items for trade. The basic food was ship's biscuit, salted meat, cheese, dried fish, and beans. There was wine and water to drink. Keeping food fresh was a problem. Many sailors died from scurvy, a disease caused by a lack of vitamin C.

Finding a good crew was also difficult. Many Spanish sailors would not work for a Portuguese commander. But, eventually, 277 men were picked. They were joined by an Italian nobleman, Antonio Pigafetta, who kept a diary of the voyage, the only account we have. At last, on September 20, 1519, the expedition set sail from Spain.

What was life like on board?

"It was very crowded and uncomfortable."

The ships in Magellan's fleet were small. The largest, the *San Antonio*, weighed 130 tons and was about 52 yards long. There was little space for rest and shelter. The captain had his own cabin above water level, but the sailors slept wherever they could find a space. When the sea was rough, water leaked through the deck and drenched the sailors.

On board, each sailor had his own job to do. The captain took charge of navigation. The master and boatswain managed the crew. Ordinary sailors were kept busy with the sails and with repairs to the ships. There were also cooks, gunners, and carpenters. Others guarded the supplies in the ship's hold. Below the hold was the bilge, which was filled with stones to help balance the ship.

High in the mainmast, sailors took turns sitting in the crow's-nest. From here, they could watch for enemy ships, bad weather, and land. At night, the ships signaled to each other with flashing lanterns.

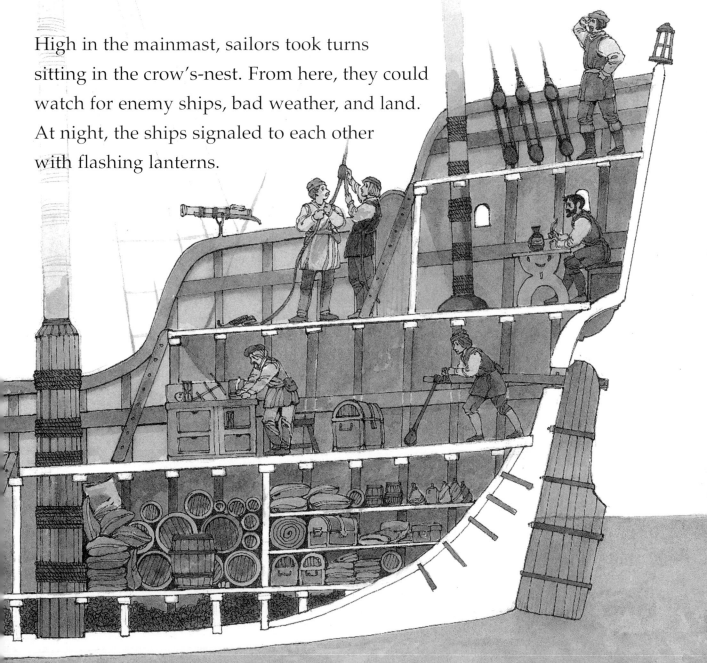

What was your worst moment?

"The worst was when three of my ships mutinied and tried to sail for home."

The ships headed south and then west across the Atlantic Ocean. They ran into storms, then drifted into the doldrums, an area of windless calm near the equator. The sun made the food rot, and melted the tar that held the timber frame together, so that the ships sprang leaks.

In early December 1519, the fleet arrived off the coast of South America. They dropped anchor at Rio de Janeiro in Brazil. The boats were repaired and fresh supplies taken on board. On Christmas Day, they set sail again, continuing south into stormy seas and icy winds. On March 31, 1520, Ferdinand took shelter in the harbor of San Julian in Patagonia.

It was there that three of the Spanish captains mutinied. Ferdinand acted quickly. With the two loyal ships, he blocked the harbor and captured the mutineers. One captain was tried and executed, one was murdered, and the third was left ashore. Their crews were ordered to work in chains.

What was the most exciting time?

"Oh, definitely when we discovered *el paso*."

Two months later, a storm drove the *San Antonio* and *Concepçion* towards rocks near the tip of South America. Just as Ferdinand gave up on the two lost ships, they reappeared, sails billowing and flags waving. The wind had blown them into a deep channel lined with high cliffs. They had found *el paso*!

Ferdinand led just three ships through the channel now named after him. (The *Santiago* had been wrecked earlier, and the *San Antonio* had deserted by now.) When they reached the other end a month later, a vast sea stretched out before them.

Ferdinand called the ocean the *Mar Pacifico*, or Peaceful Sea, but his joy was short-lived. Week after week, there was still no land in sight. The crew ate old ship's biscuit full of grubs and drank yellow, stinking water. One by one, the men started to die.

On March 6, 1521, after four exhausting months, the survivors finally reached the beautiful island of Guam in the Mariana Islands, 1,200 miles east of the Philippines. They were saved!

How did you find the way?

"We had many special instruments to help us."

Ferdinand was a great navigator. He found his way across waters no European had sailed before. The charts that he made, helped mapmakers to show the true size of the Pacific Ocean.

Ferdinand used a compass to plot the ship's course and direction. He then checked his position against the position of the stars. His sailors also used instruments called quadrants and astrolabes to measure the height of the sun or the polestar above the horizon. This helped them find how far north or south of the equator they were. But they had no way of knowing how far east or west they had sailed, so they were never certain where they were.

To measure time, they used hourglasses filled with "sand" made from powdered eggshell. The hourglass was turned over every two hours to time the watches that made up a sailor's day. Each watch lasted for four hours.

What happened next?

"The fleet sailed on to the Philippines."

After three days in Guam, the fleet set sail again. Ten days later, they reached the Philippine Islands. At first, their stay was peaceful. The local people traded gold, pearls, and precious stones for the sailors' mirrors, knives, and combs. Ferdinand claimed the islands for Spain. But then disaster struck.

Ferdinand found himself drawn into a war between two islands. On April 27, he set out with 60 men in three rowing boats to attack the island of Mactan. They were met by hundreds of angry Mactans. The battle raged for hours, until Ferdinand told his men to retreat. As he waded back to his boat, he was slashed across the leg with a sword and fell face down in the sea. His Spanish officers made little effort to help him.

In seconds, his body had been cut to pieces. It was a tragic end for such a great man.

Homeward bound

After Ferdinand's death, the Spanish officers took the *Trinidad* and *Victoria* and sailed south to the Spice Islands. Soon afterward, the *Trinidad* sprang a leak, and the *Victoria* traveled on alone under the command of Captain Juan Sebastian del Cano. On September 6, 1522, almost exactly three years after they left, the *Victoria* sailed up the river to Seville. The ship was barely afloat. Out of the original company of 277 men, there were only 18 survivors.

They had sailed right around the world, a distance of almost 44,000 miles. It was the longest journey ever made. The sailors themselves got little thanks and were never fully paid for their services. Meanwhile, the mutineers spread lies about Ferdinand. Only Antonio Pigafetta, the Italian nobleman, recognized Magellan's brilliance as a leader and navigator.

Many years later, Magellan finally achieved the fame he deserved for making one of the greatest voyages of discovery possible.

Some important dates

1480 Ferdinand Magellan is born in Sabrosa, Portugal. This is the Age of Exploration, with Spain and Portugal leading the way.

1492 Christopher Columbus sails from Spain to America. Magellan is sent to Lisbon to become a page.

1493 The Treaty of Tordesillas divides the world in half, between Portugal and Spain.

1498 Vasco da Gama, a navigator from Portugal, discovers a new route to India from Europe.

1505 After many requests to the king, Magellan goes to sea for the first time, on an expedition to weaken Arab control of the spice trade. He is wounded in battle.

1512 Magellan reaches the Philippines by sailing east.

1513 Magellan volunteers for service fighting in Morocco. He is wounded in the leg and left with a limp for the rest of his life.

1516 Magellan wants to lead an expedition to the Philippines and Spice Islands, this time sailing west. King Manuel of Portugal refuses to help him.

1517 Magellan leaves Portugal for Spain. King Charles I agrees to provide ships and supplies for Magellan's voyage.

1517 Magellan marries Beatriz Barbosa, a Spanish official's daughter. They have a son, Rodrigo.

1519 In September, Magellan's fleet of five ships leaves Seville.

In December 1519, the ships enter the bay of Rio de Janeiro in Brazil.

1520 In March, the fleet takes shelter in San Julian, Patagonia, for the winter (south of the equator, the seasons are reversed). The sailors are the first Europeans to see penguins and seals.

In April 1520, Magellan crushes a mutiny at San Julian.

The *Santiago* is wrecked while exploring along the coastline.

In October 1520, Magellan finds *el paso*. The *San Antonio* turns around and sails for home, but the rest of the fleet sails through. They are the first Europeans to see the Pacific Ocean, the largest ocean in the world. *El paso* is later named the Strait of Magellan.

1521 In March, the fleet reaches Guam, in the Mariana Islands. From there, they sail to the Philippine Islands.

In April 1521, Magellan gets involved in a local war and is killed on the island of Mactan. The Spanish officers burn Magellan's papers and set sail. They leave the *Concepçion* behind because it has been badly damaged by shipworms.

In November 1521, the *Trinidad* and the *Victoria* reach the Spice Islands.

1522 In September, one ship, the *Victoria*, and 18 men return to Seville, having sailed around the world. Antonio Pigafetta is among the survivors. His diary gives us the only accurate account of the voyage written at the time.

The *Victoria's* commander, Juan Sebastian del Cano, is rewarded with a new coat of arms from the king. Magellan's achievements are ignored, and del Cano gets all the glory from the voyage.

Glossary

astronomy The study of the sun, moon, stars, and planets.

bilge The very bottom part of a ship.

Catholic faith The Christian faith based on the teachings and rules of the Roman Catholic Church. It has the Pope as its head.

chart A kind of map that helped people find their way at sea.

cockroach A large beetle.

docks A place in a harbor where ships can be unloaded and loaded.

doldrums A dangerous area for sailing ships, where there is hardly any wind or no wind at all.

expedition An organized journey with a special purpose, such as scientific discovery.

flagship The ship that the commander of a fleet sails in.

fleet Several ships sailing together.

hourglass A timer made from two glass funnels joined in the middle. Fine sand falls from one side to the other over a period of time.

hold The space in a ship for storing supplies and cargo.

hull The outer body of a ship.

mutiny To rebel or go against a leader's command.

navigation The skill of planning the route a ship, plane, or car takes. A **navigator** is a person who is skilled in navigation.

noble Someone who belongs to a group of people who have titles, such as lord, lady, or duke.

page A boy trained to serve nobles, especially at a royal court.

Philippines Islands in Southeast Asia, also called the Philippine Islands.

port A town or city by the sea.

route A way followed from one place to another, by sea or land. A trade route is one that traders follow from one country to another.

scurvy A disease suffered by sailors in the past and caused by lack of fresh fruit and vegetables in their diet. Symptoms of the disease included swollen gums and a rash. Victims usually died.

ship's biscuit A very hard, tasteless cracker, eaten by sailors.

shipyards A place where ships are built and repaired.

Spice Islands Islands in Indonesia, now called the Moluccas.

spices Plants, or part of some plants, that are used to flavor food. In Magellan's day, spices were also used to keep meat and other food from going bad. They were very expensive to buy.

strait A water channel that connects two seas.

treaty An agreement between countries or states.

Vasco da Gama (?1469–1524) A Portuguese navigator who led an expedition to discover the sea route from Portugal to India, sailing around South Africa.

voyage A long journey by sea.

watch A period of time in which someone keeps guard.

Index